MW01518974

CVC
Word Families
Cut, Spell and Paste

Little Scholar

© CVC Word Families: Cut, Spell and Paste. All rights reserved. No part of this publication may be reproduced, distributed or transmitted, in any form or by any means, including photocopying, without the written permission of the publisher.

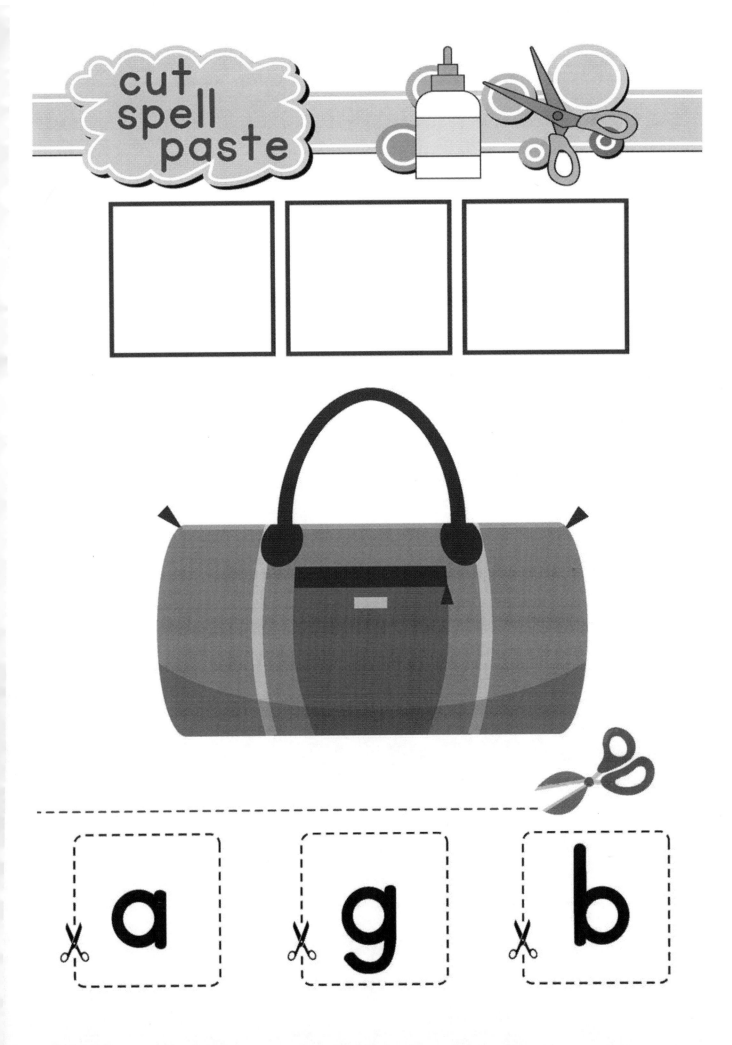

cut
spell
paste

g   r   a

cut
spell
paste

$4

a + g

a   w   g

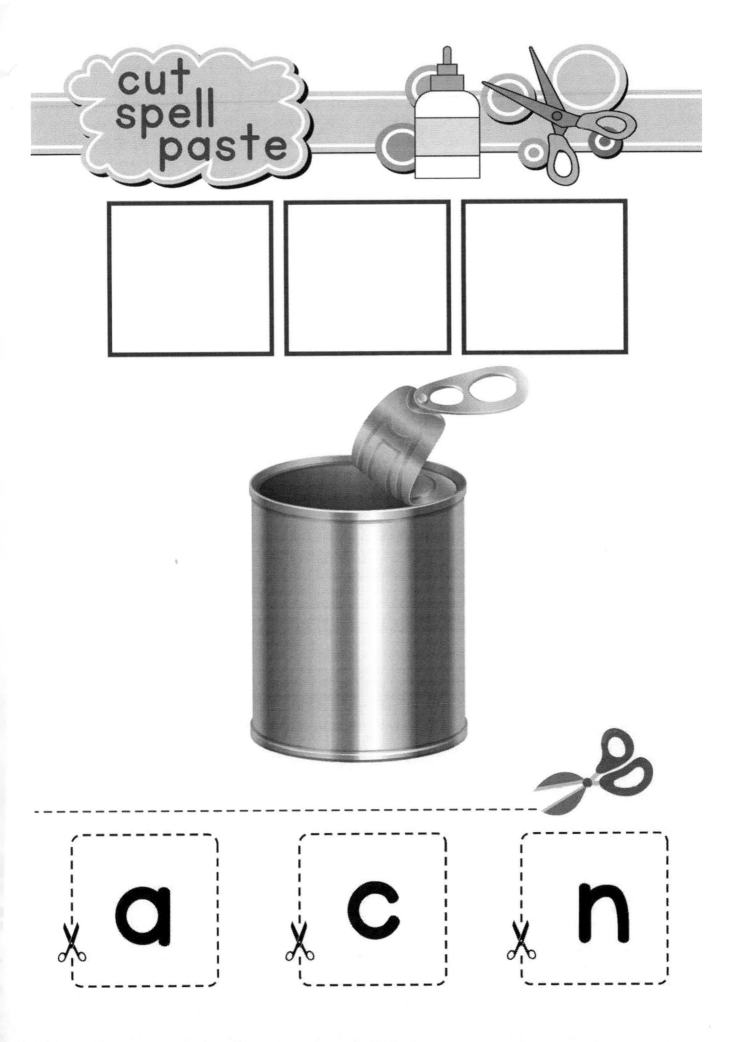

cut
spell
paste

a c n

cut
spell
paste

f n a

m   n   a

cut
spell
paste

p n a

cut
spell
paste

v n a

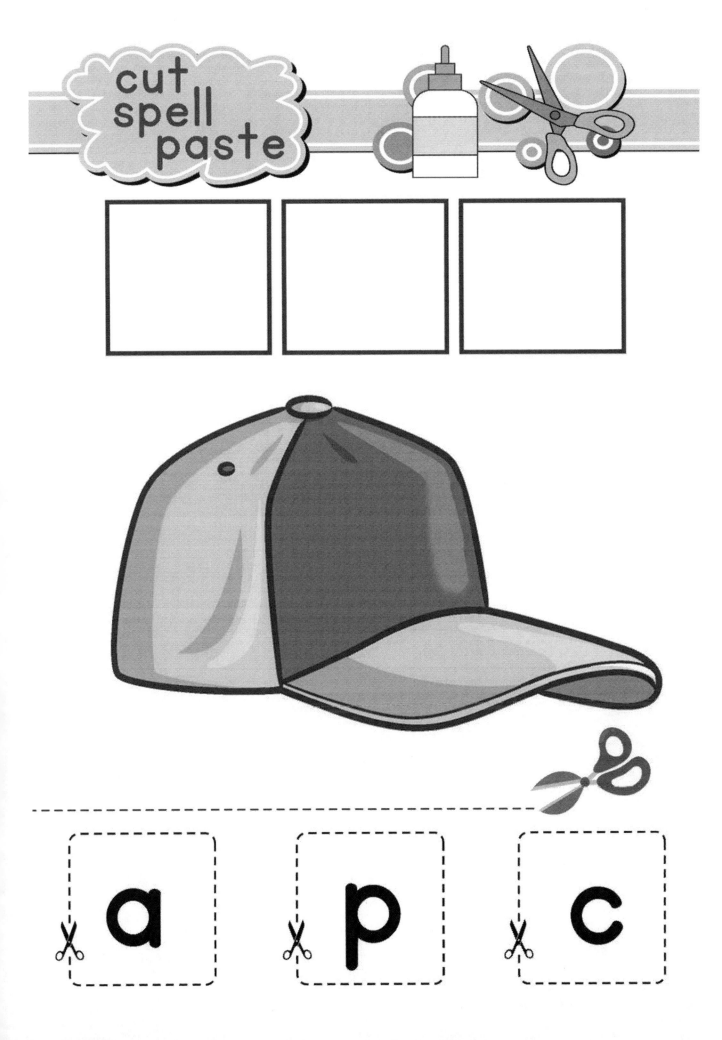

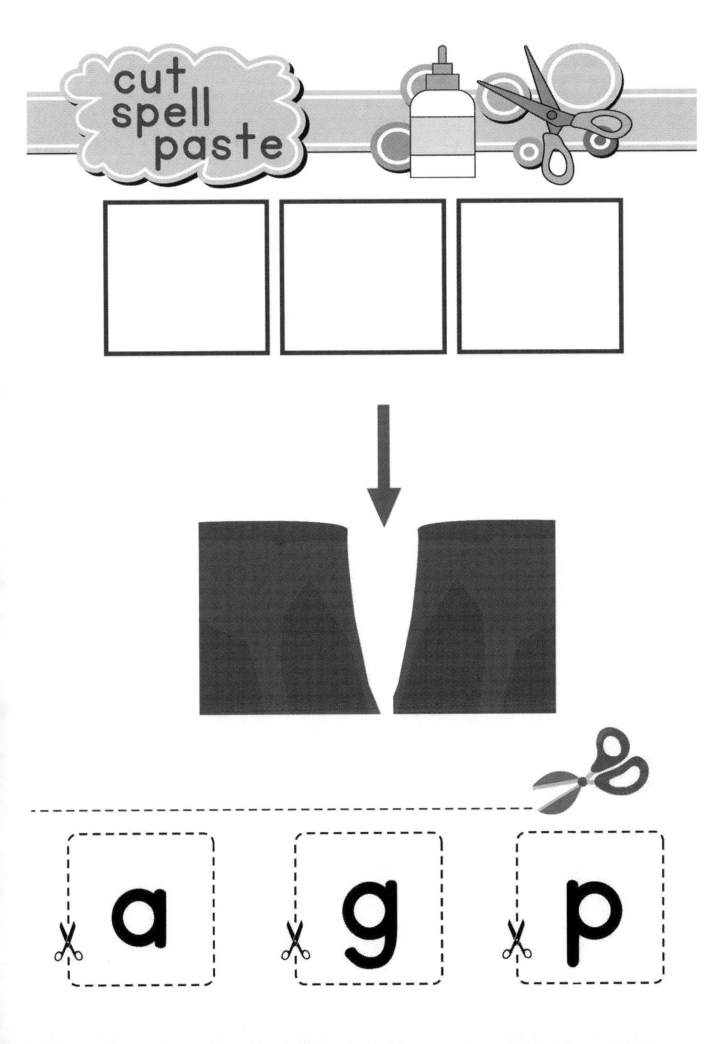

cut
spell
paste

a g p

cut
spell
paste

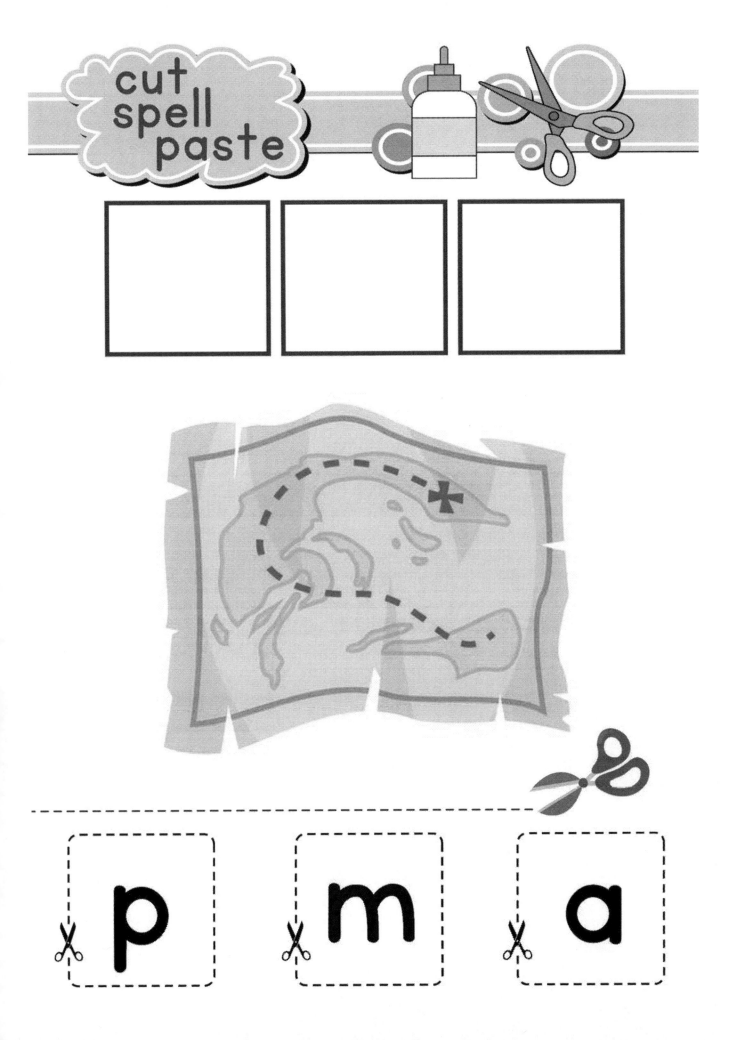

cut
spell
paste

p   m   a

cut
spell
paste

n p a

cut
spell
paste

p   t   a

cut
spell
paste

TAXI

c b a

cut
spell
paste

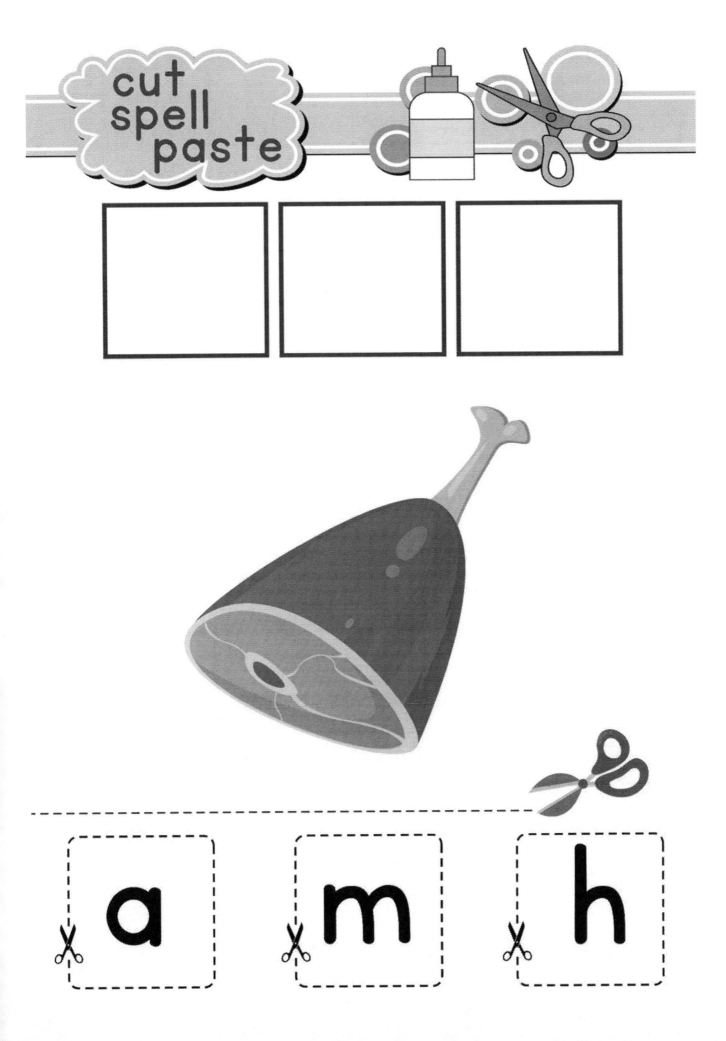

cut
spell
paste

a   m   h

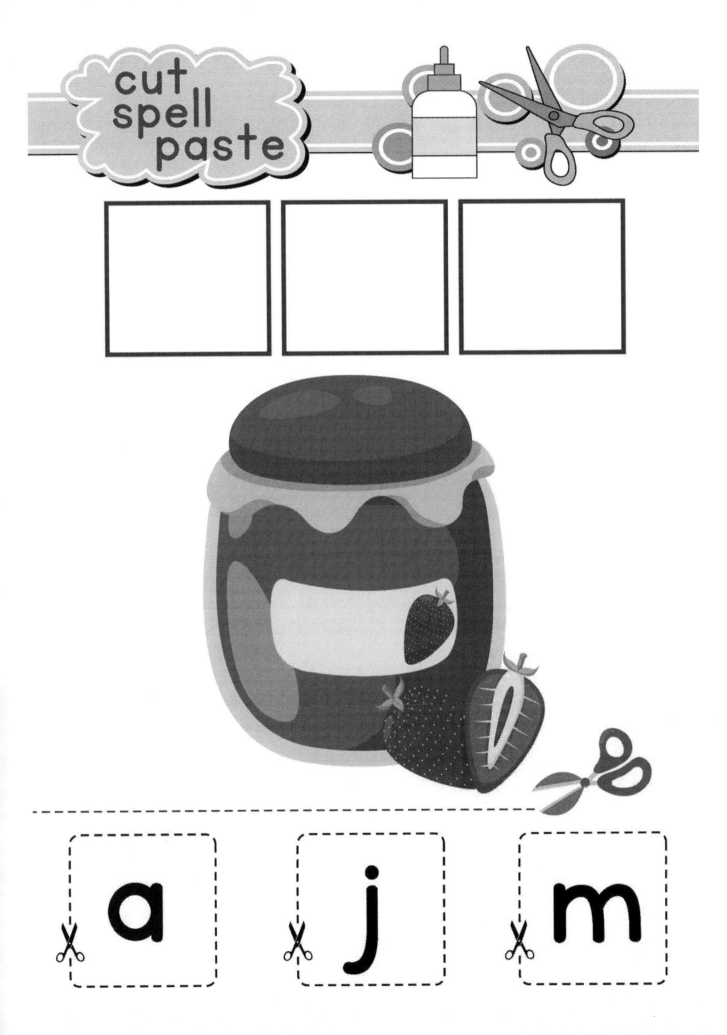

a   j   m

m   r   a

k   y   a

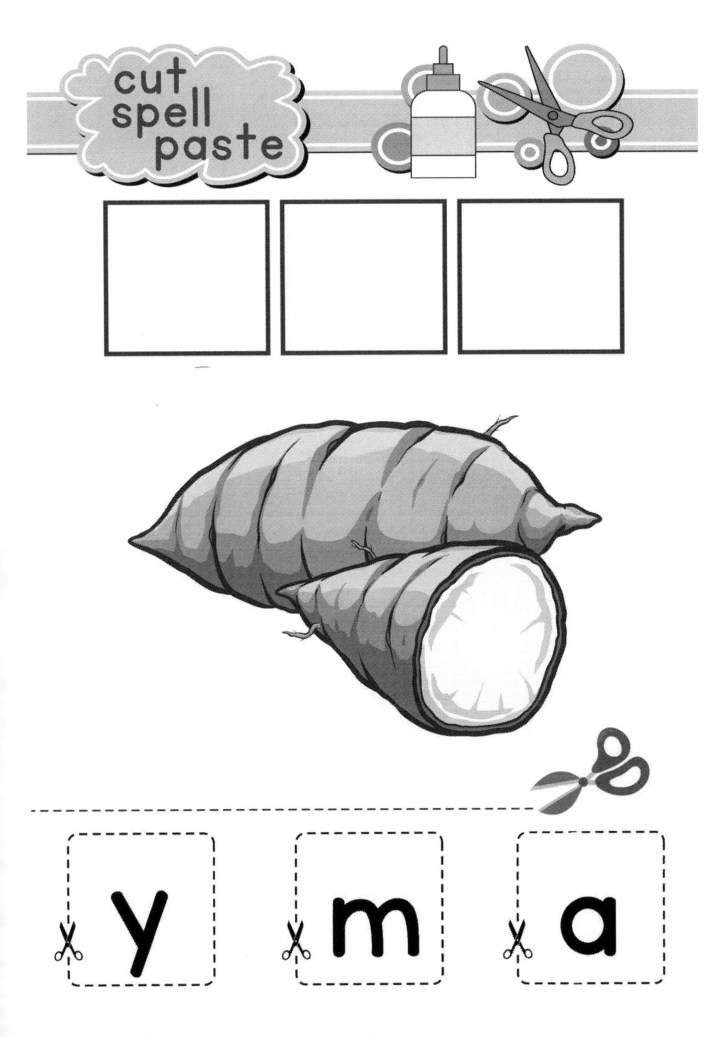

cut
spell
paste

y m a

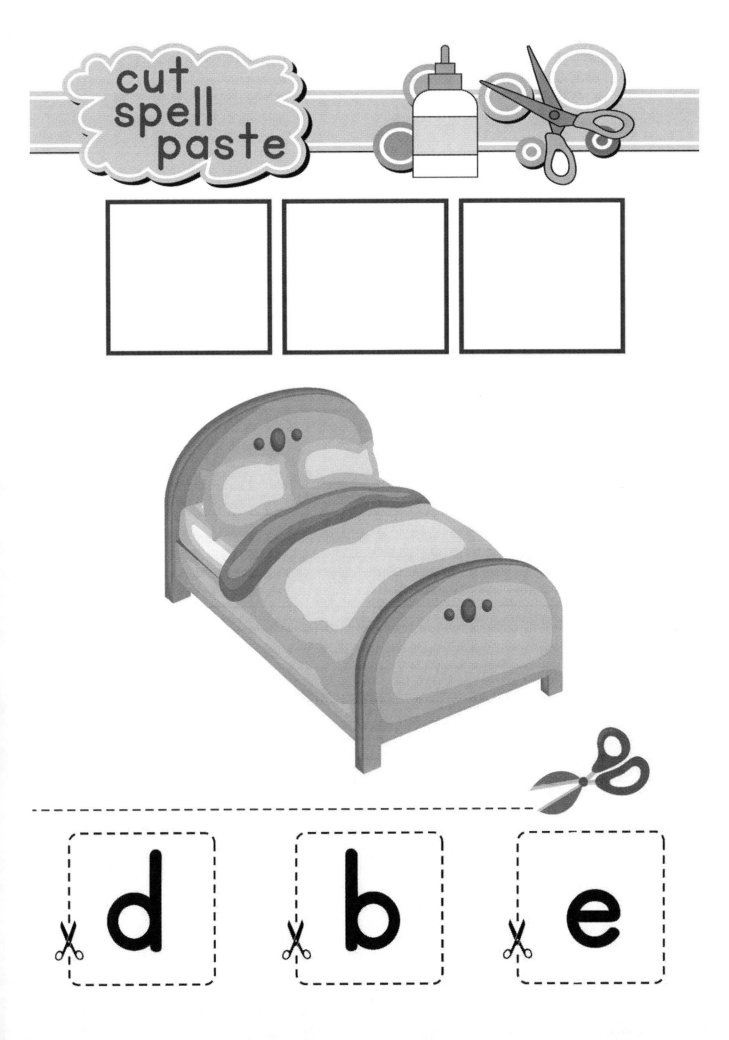

cut
spell
paste

d   b   e

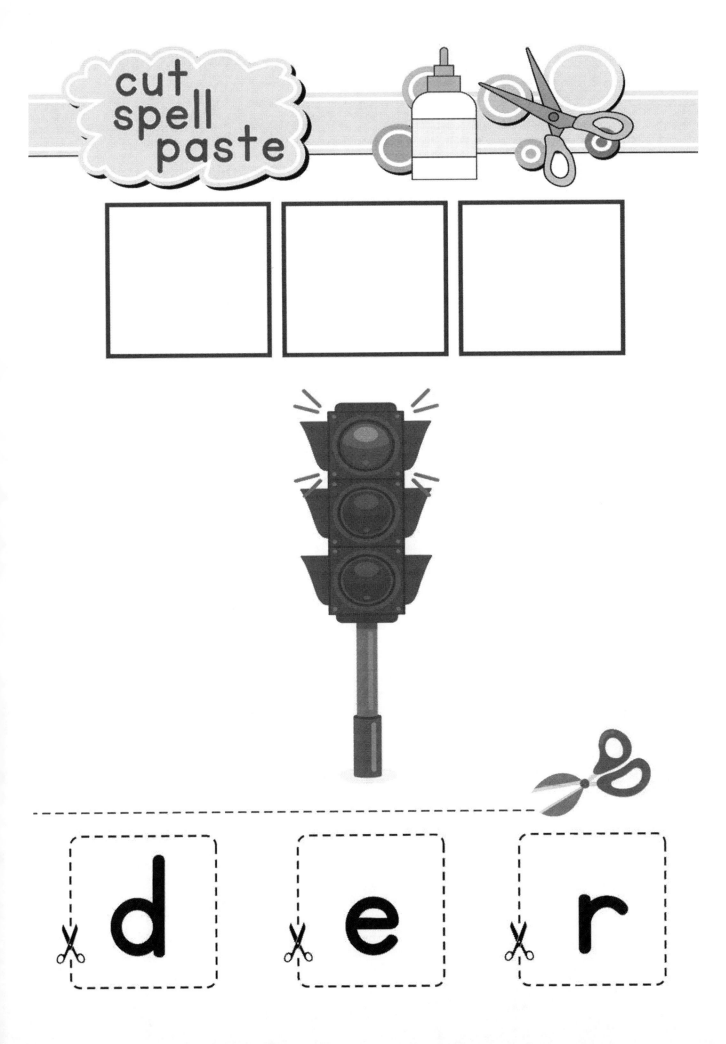

d e r

cut
spell
paste

b g e

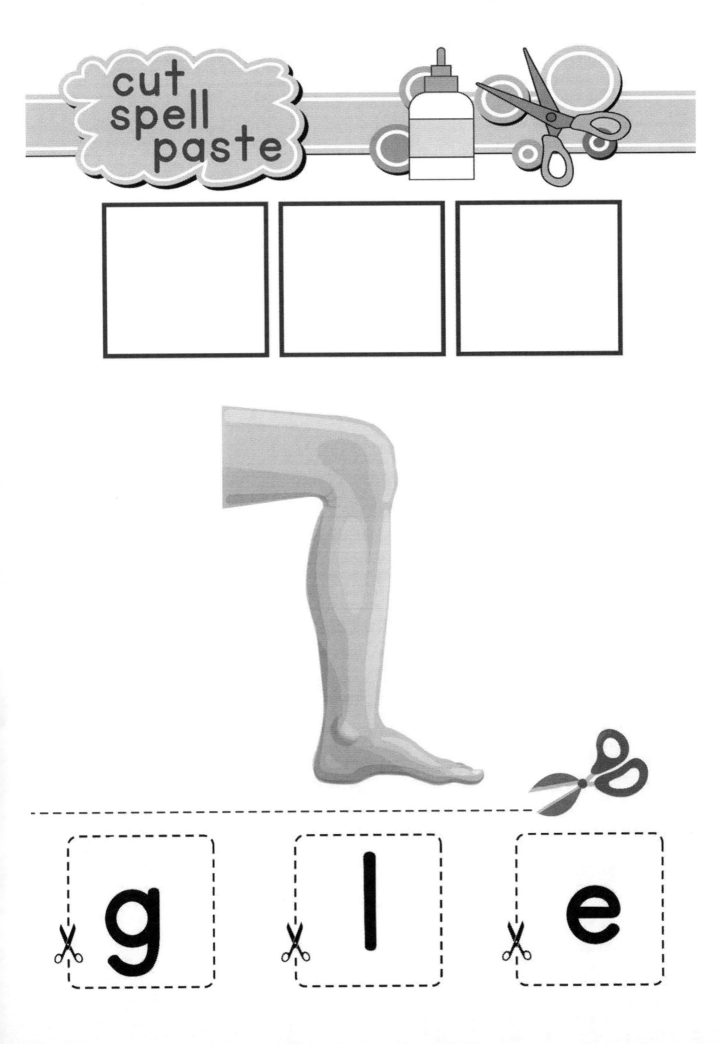

g   l   e

h   n   e

cut
spell
paste

e   n   m

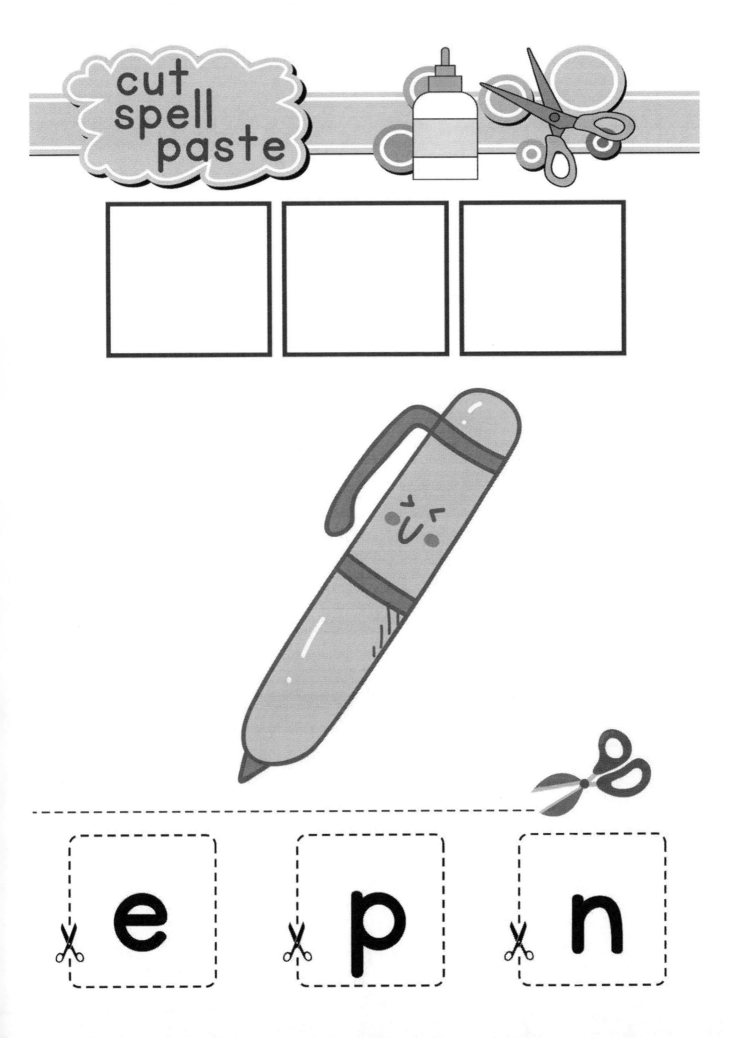

e   p   n

cut
spell
paste

10

e   t   n

cut
spell
paste

t e g

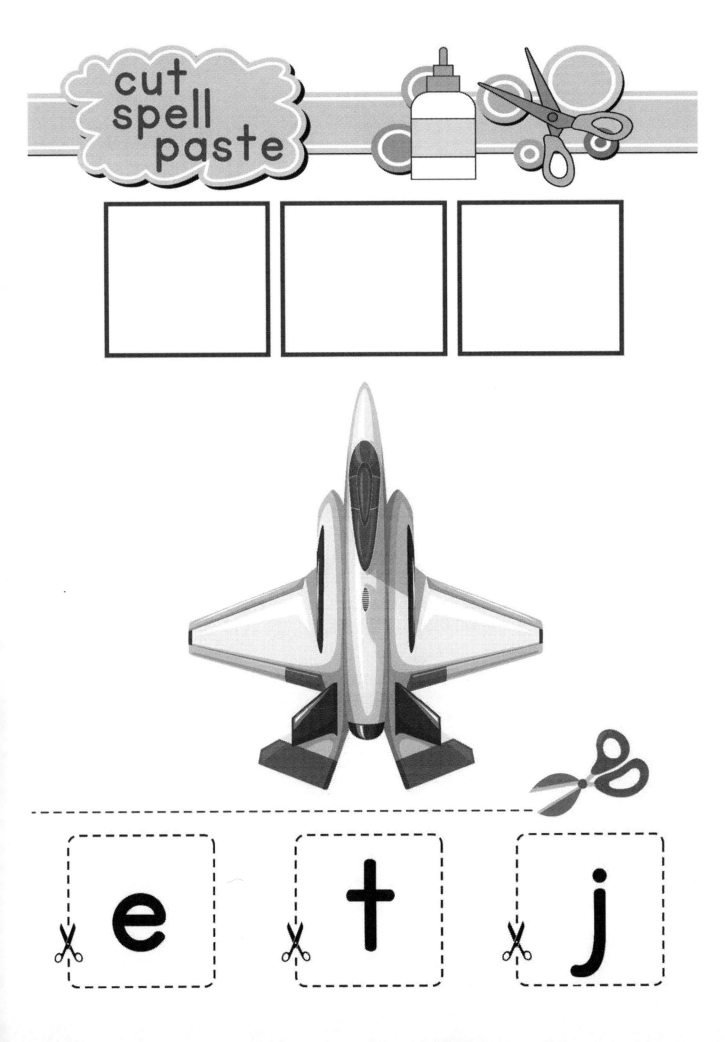

cut
spell
paste

e   t   j

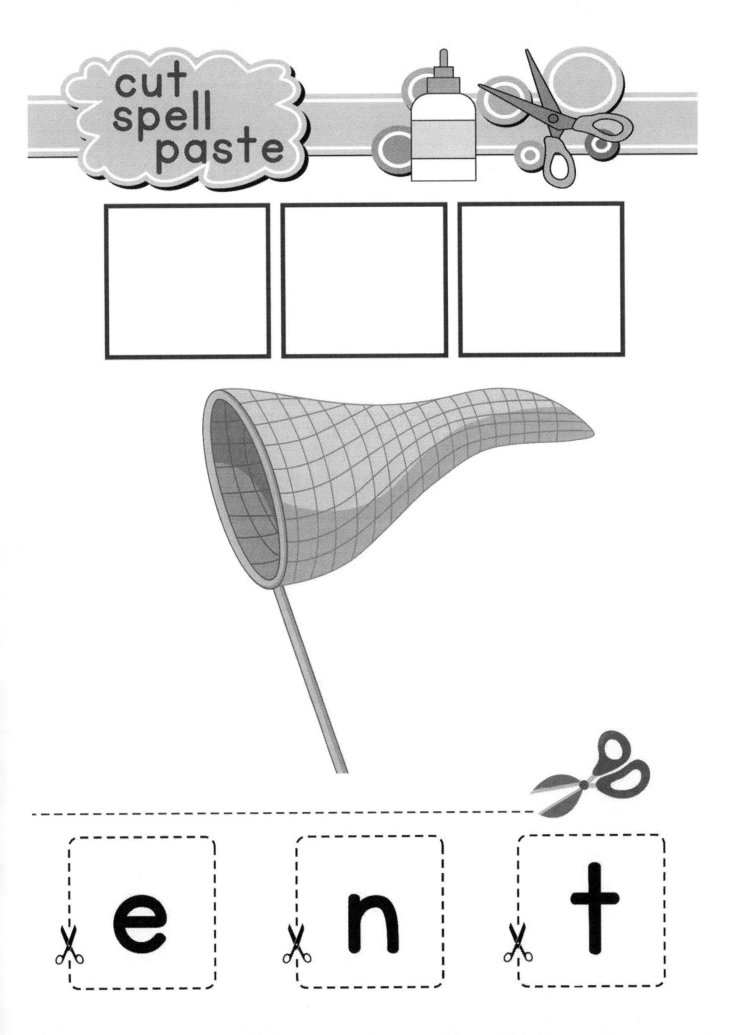

cut
spell
paste

e n t

cut
spell
paste

t   v   e

cut
spell
paste

w t e

b w e

i

h

d

cut
spell
paste

i d k

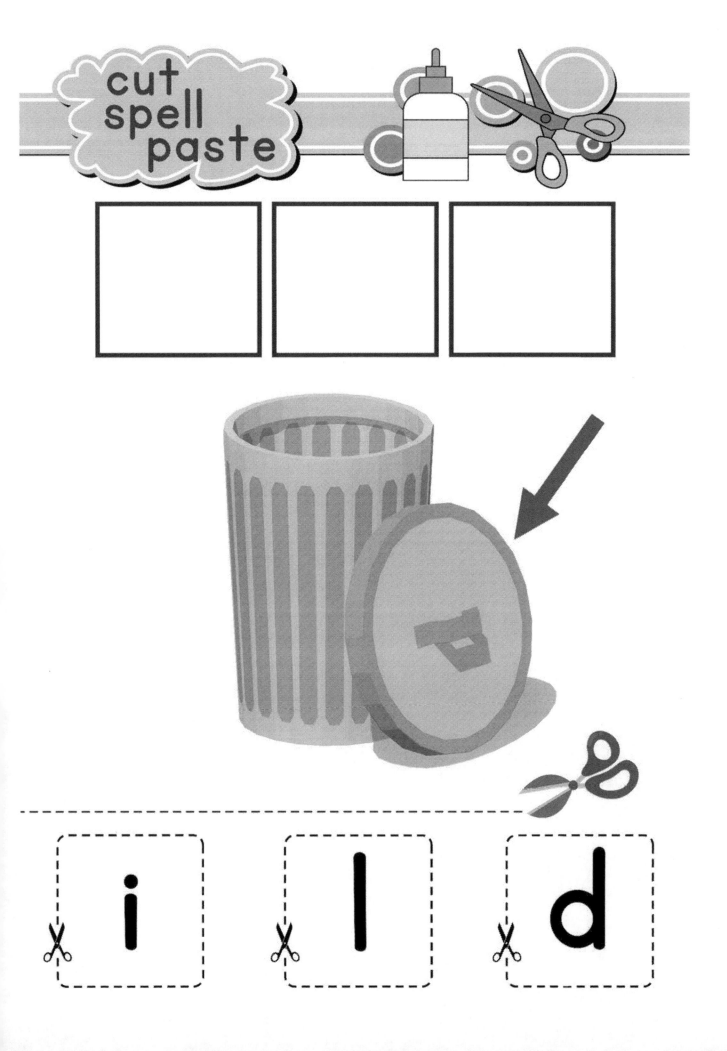

cut
spell
paste

i l d

cut
spell
paste

b   g   i

cut
spell
paste

g   d   i

g   i   f

cut
spell
paste

g   p   i

cut
spell
paste

i w g

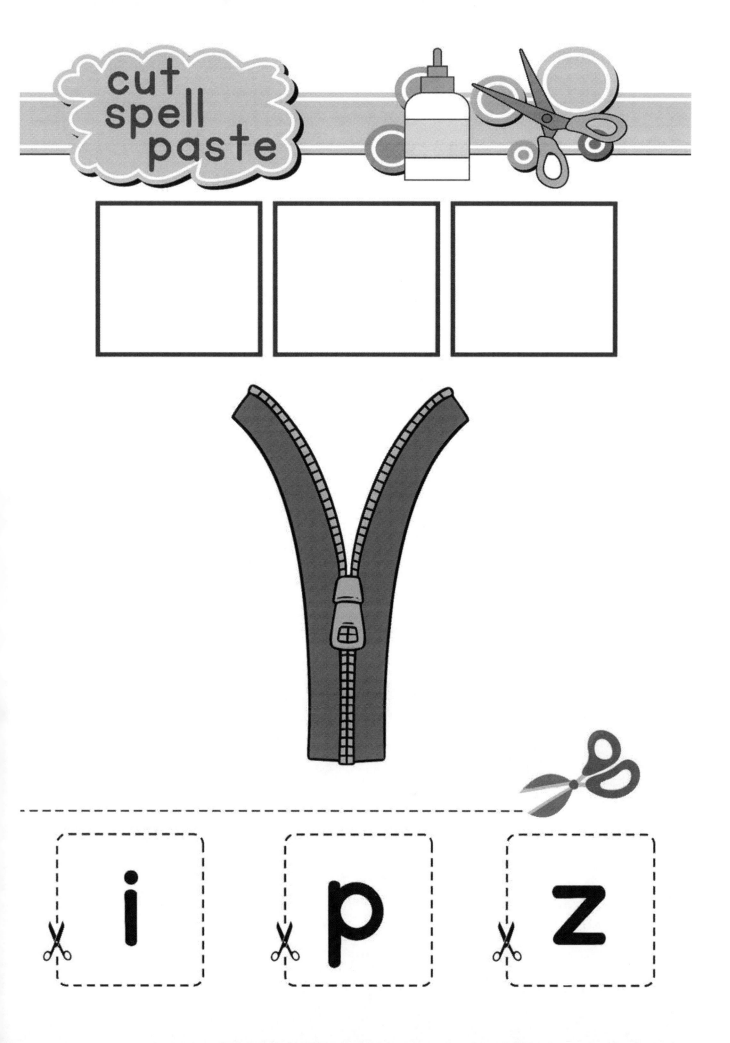

cut
spell
paste

i p z

cut
spell
paste

t   i   h

cut
spell
paste

i p t

cut
spell
paste

t

s

i

cut
spell
paste

o   b   s

cut
spell
paste

o d g

cut
spell
paste

f g o

h   g   o

cut
spell
paste

o   j   g

cut
spell
paste

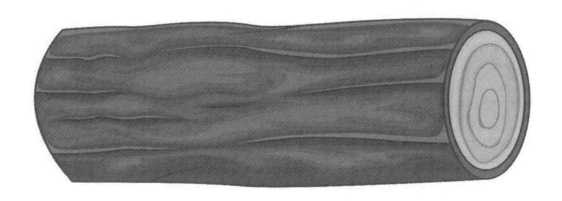

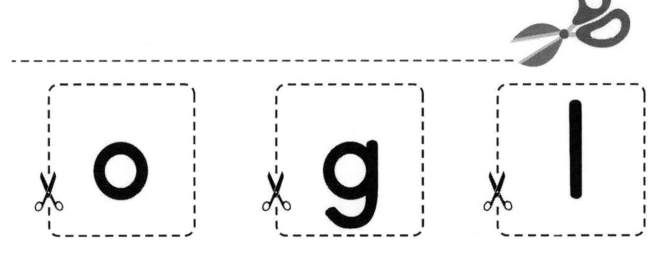

o   g   l

cut
spell
paste

o   c   p

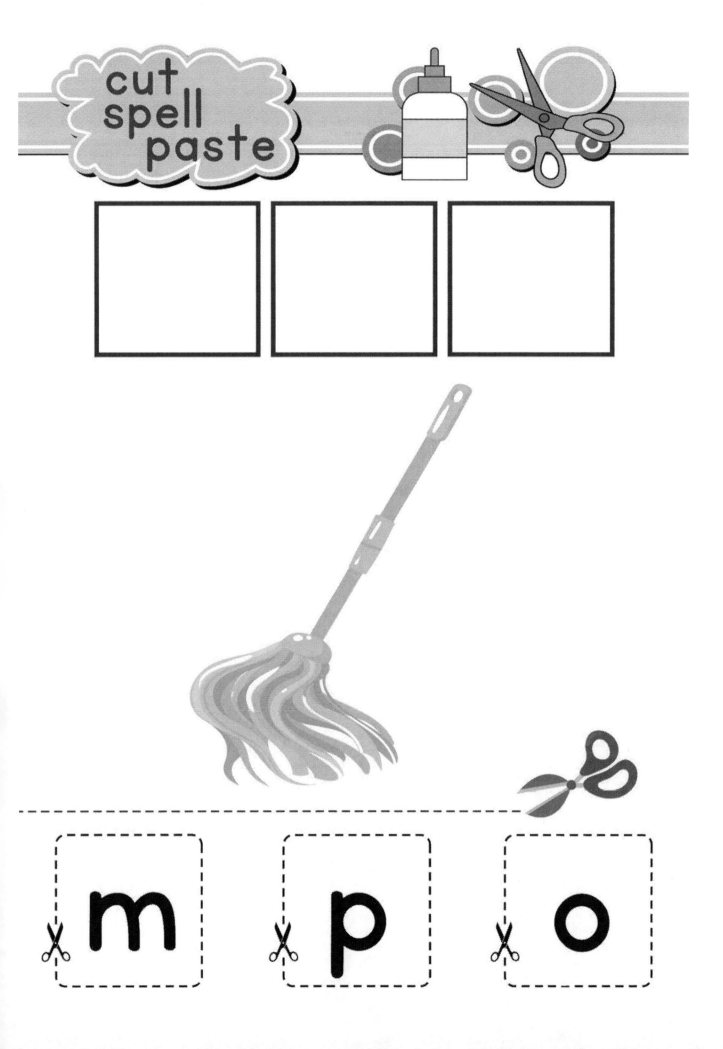

cut
spell
paste

m p o

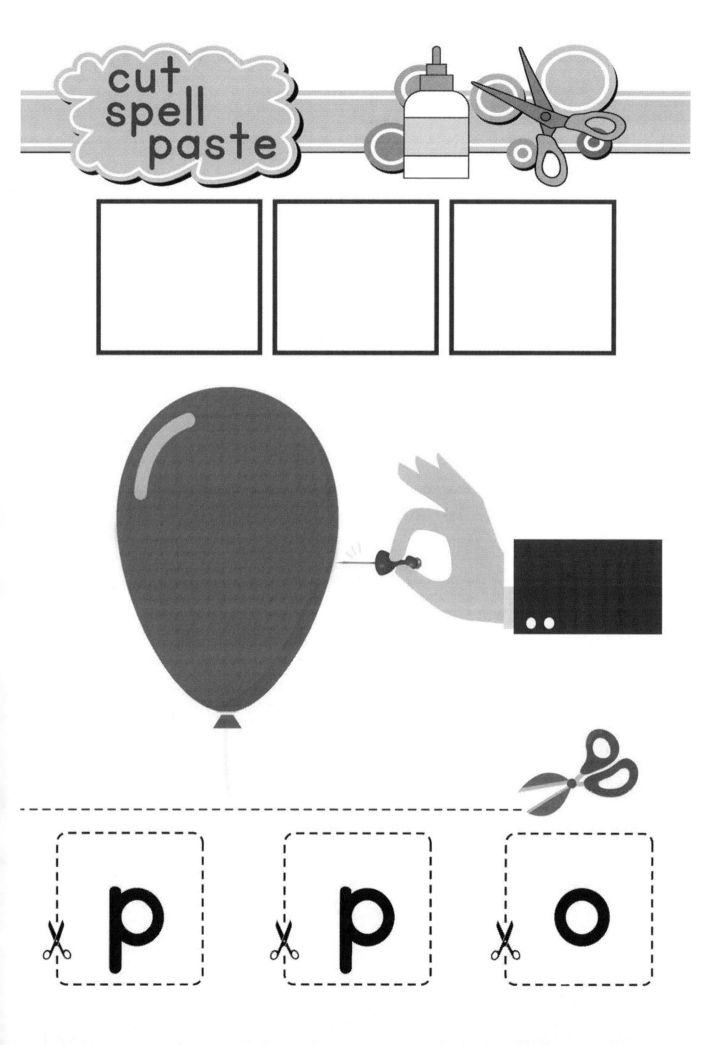

cut
spell
paste

p p o

cut
spell
paste

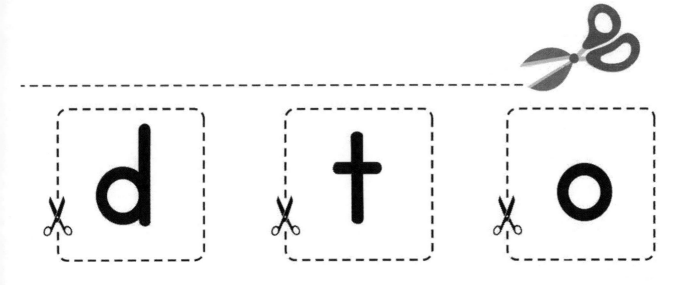

d   t   o

cut
spell
paste

o   t   h

cut
spell
paste

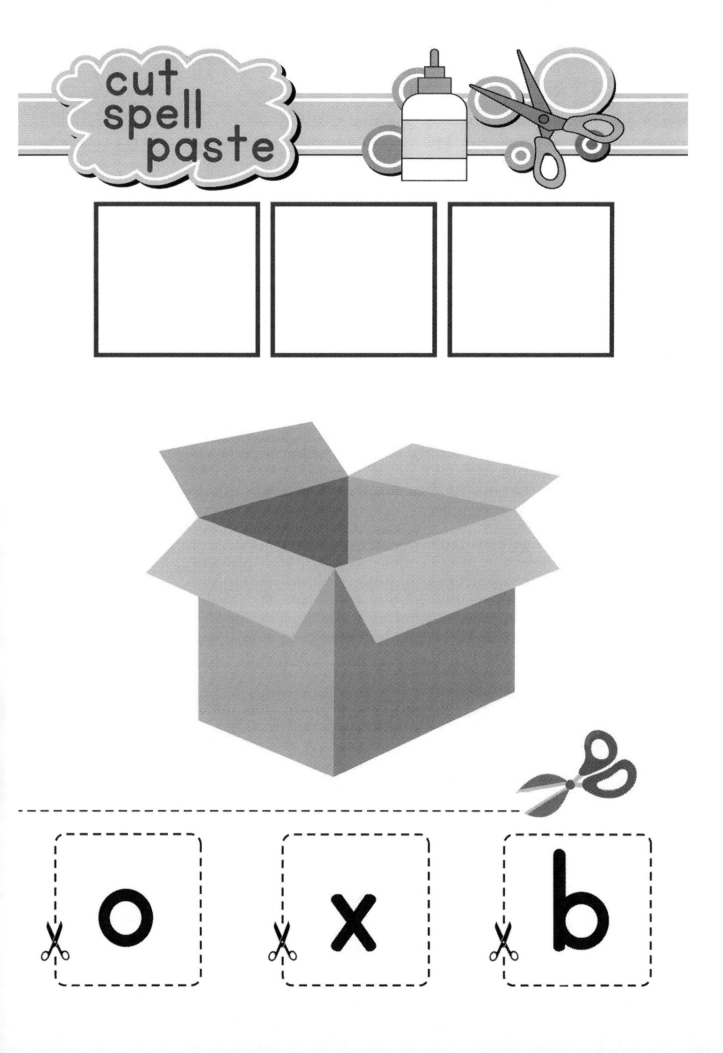

cut
spell
paste

cut
spell
paste

x
f
o

cut
spell
paste

b   c   u

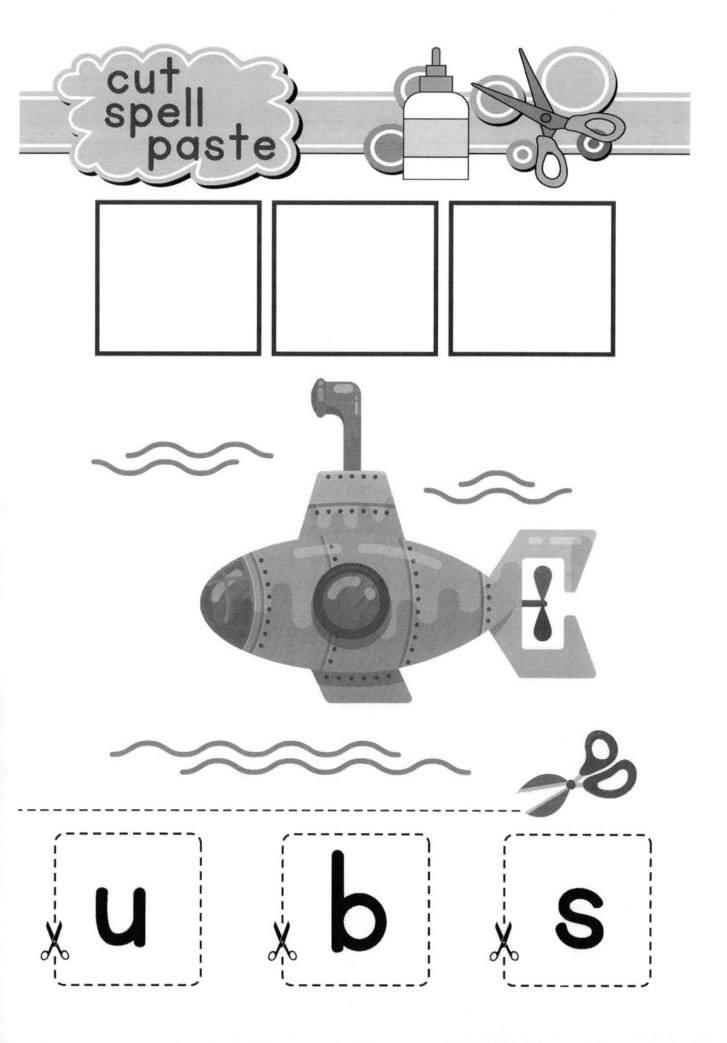

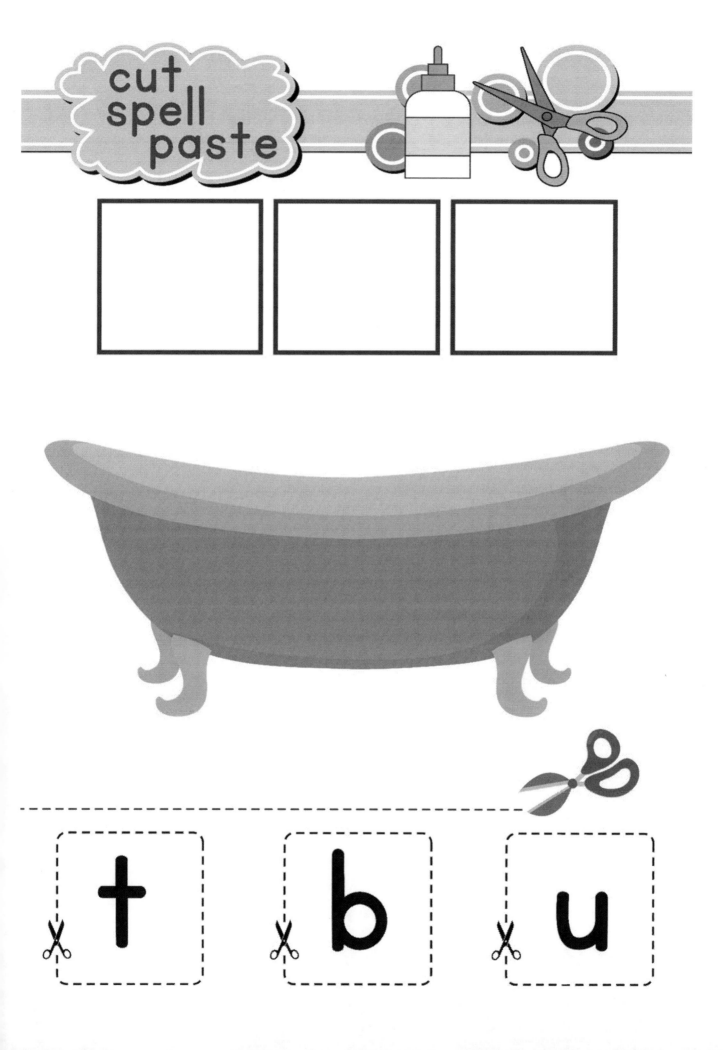

cut
spell
paste

t   b   u

cut
spell
paste

u   h   g

cut
spell
paste

j g u

cut
spell
paste

m   g   u

cut
spell
paste

g

r

u

cut
spell
paste

b n u

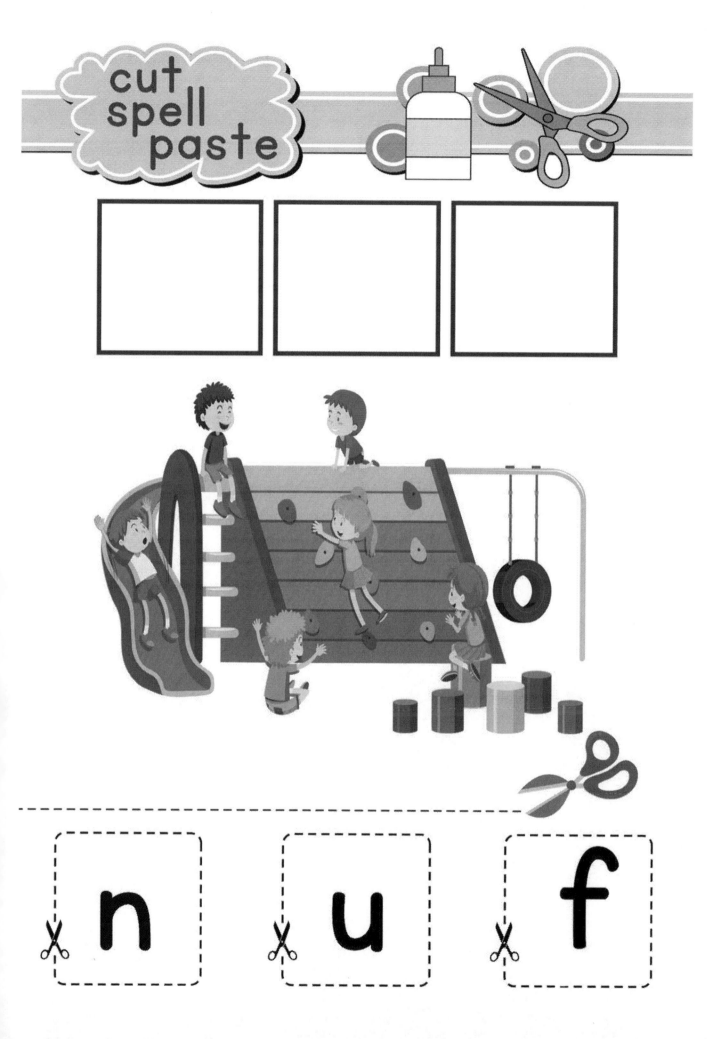

n

u

f

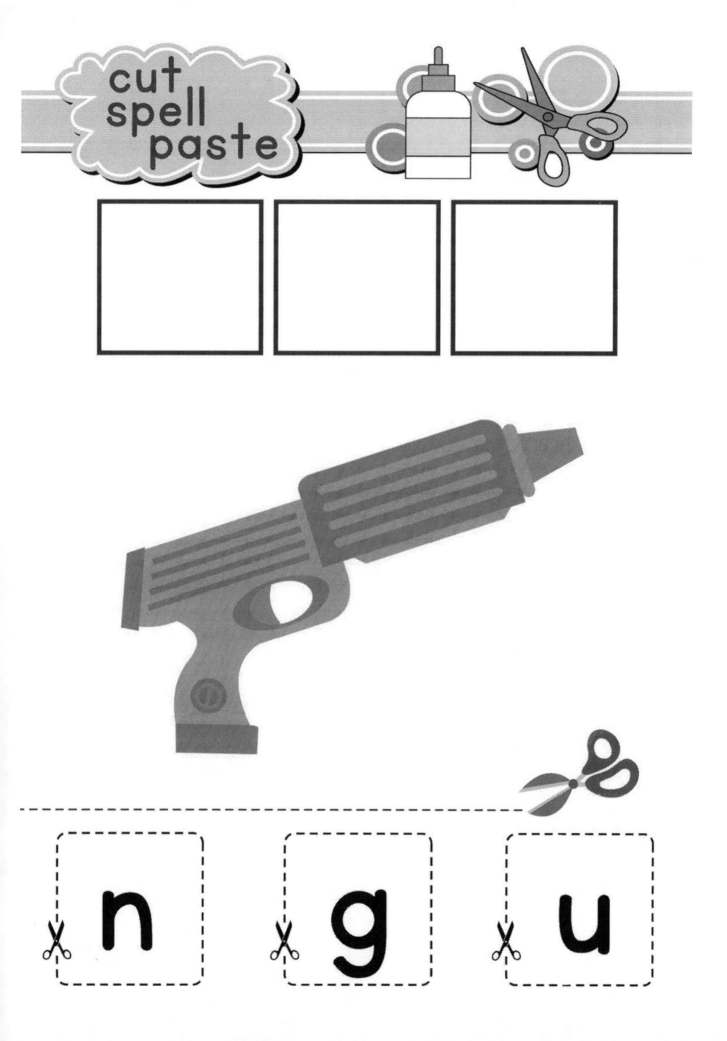

cut
spell
paste

n g u

cut
spell
paste

n   u   r

cut
spell
paste

n   s   u

cut
spell
paste

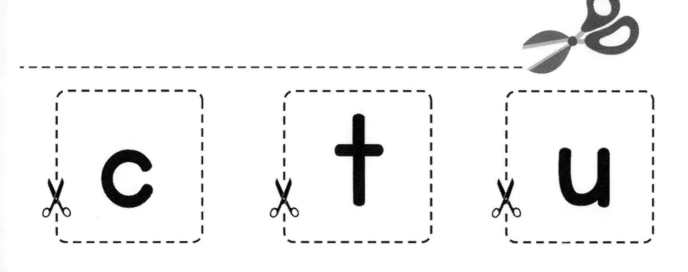

t

h

u

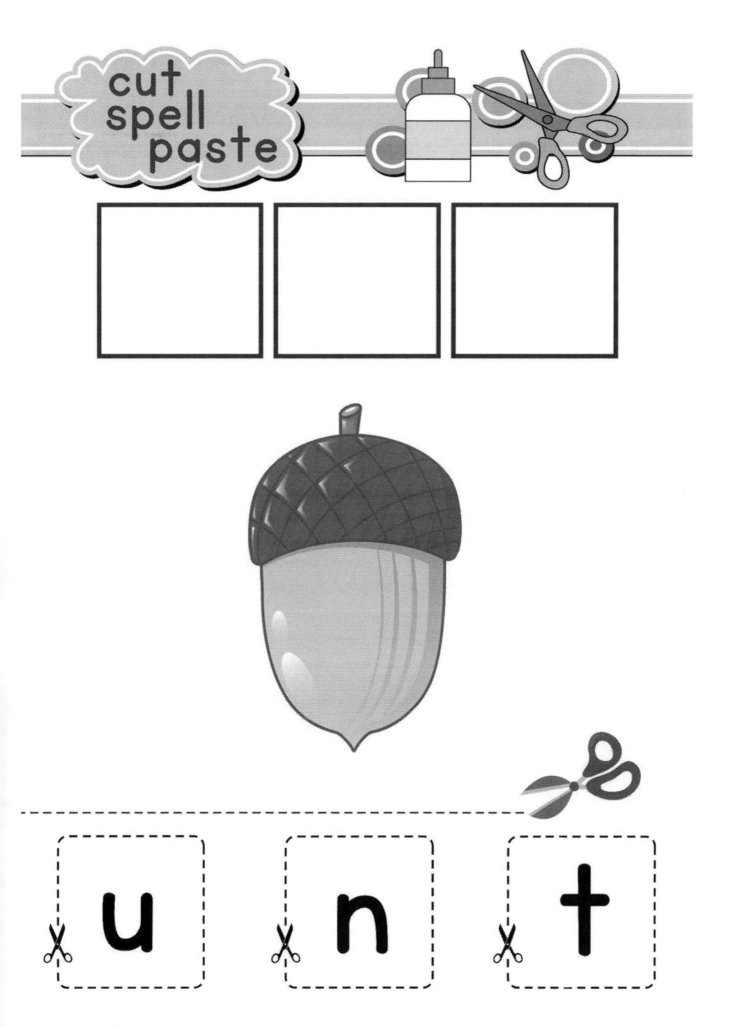

cut
spell
paste

cut
spell
paste

d   m   u

cut
spell
paste

u   p   c

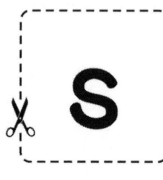

We would love to hear your honest opinion about this book.

Please, leave a review.

https://www.amazon.com/dp/B089M1FF9X

Manufactured by Amazon.ca
Bolton, ON

35799257R00111